BLACK
Excellence

IDENTIFYING YOUR
SUPERPOWER
And Becoming A Top Achiever

PROFESSOR GEORGE C. HAIRSTON

Copyright © 2023 by Professor George C. Hairston.

Publisher: Quantum Leap Media Group

ISBN: 979-8-9881674-1-9

All rights reserved. No part of this book may be reproduced or transmitted in any form or by any means, electronic or mechanical, including photocopying, recording, or by any information storage and retrieval system, without permission in writing from the copyright owner.

This book was printed in the United States of America.

FOREWORD

DR. BYRON WILLIAMS

When Professor George Hairston asked me to write this foreword for his book, I was initially astonished and anxious. I felt that I could not provide an appropriate commentary on his work. But as I thought about it, I realized that I am a product of his God-driven mission to inspire Black Excellence.

I often speak of my encounter with Professor Hairston as my "Road to Damascus experience." In the New Testament of the Bible, the Apostle Paul (then known as Saul) underwent a dramatic transformation and gained insight into his purpose in life.

While recruiting for a college in the summer of 2010, Professor Hairston approached me for what I thought was a recruiting conversation. By the end of our conversation, he enlightened me that God had more for me to accomplish. At that point in my life, I was content with having a job, completing my bachelor's degree, and being retired from the military.

Reflecting on Professor Hairston's work concerning Black Excellence, it tells the story of top-achieving Black people who understand the value of pouring wisdom into the next generation. That means supporting Black Excellence through flaws and imperfections while understanding that the purpose still has time to develop and make a significant impact in one's life.

Not only will Professor Hairston utilize his God-given mission and superpowers to push you into your excellence, but he is gifted in encouraging you to be prepared for greatness. His former students continually referred to him as Professor Hairston, not just for his academic achievements but also for his ability to assist others in achieving excellence in their lives.

What defines someone as a professor? One who professes, avows, or declares or professes special knowledge of an art, sport, or occupation requiring skill. One conversation with Professor Hairston will trigger a positive change in your life.

He lives by the example set in his book, not to boast or brag about his accomplishments or gifts, but to share the Black excellence that has been instilled in each one of us. Professor Hairston has the ability, in one single conversation, to lead you to refocus on your goals and dreams. He is a living example of Black Excellence in action.

This book on Black Excellence serves as a blueprint for utilizing your God-gifted talents to ignite change not only in your purpose but also to teach others to overcome life's obstacles and become change agents in their community.

Dr. Byron J. Williams, Author of "The PROMISE is still Valid" and "These Ashes Will Not Define My Purpose," www.DrByronJWilliams.com.

PREFACE

It was unexpected, unbelievable and now seemingly a miracle that I and many others of Black African lineage were able to accomplish so much in life, given our underprivileged backgrounds and the vast number of obstacles and barriers we faced.

It is truly amazing and almost miraculous that individuals of Black African descent, including myself, have accomplished so much despite being born into underprivileged circumstances and facing numerous obstacles and barriers. I feel fortunate and blessed to have reached 80 years of age and have my sights set on living to 100! My life has been filled with struggles and successes, and at this stage, I consider it a great and joyful success. How did I arrive at this perspective? To me, a good way to measure success in life is to reflect on your starting point, assess where you are currently, and envision where you could end up.

I am a Black African American, with DNA linking me to the Black Moor people of West Africa. I was the eleventh of twelve children, born and raised in the small farming village of Cascade, Virginia, where my family grew crops such as tobacco, corn, wheat, potatoes, tomatoes, beans, turnip greens, cabbage, and sweet potatoes. We also owned chickens, cows, pigs, and mules. Our home, along with another, was situated deep in the woods on my grandfather Joe's property, approximately one mile from the nearest highway. Whenever it rained, the long, steep, red dirt road to our home would become very slippery, forcing my father to park his old car half a mile away on flat land at the top of the hill. Nevertheless, we were content because, compared to many of our Black neighbors, we had far more. My eleven siblings, parents, and I had a home, enough food to eat, and a car that provided essential transportation.

I have many fond memories of my childhood, from the ages of four to thirteen. Two, in particular, stand out because they were frightening. The first was my mother's fear of snakes, which was so great that she considered every snake a threat to our lives. There were many types of snakes near our home, including several deadly poisonous ones. I recall that, on one occasion, she screamed and threw a magazine in the air after coming across a picture of a snake while flipping through it. Looking back, I realize that my mother's fear of snakes saved our lives.

The second fear was more abstract and instilled in me by both of my parents and my Grandma Flippen. It has had an impact on me throughout my life. It was a fear of being a Black person living in a village permeated by bigotry, hatred, and complete racial segregation, led by White Supremacists and the Ku Klux Klan (KKK). They were active, widespread, and held almost all positions of ownership and control in our village. Although a few kind and supportive White families lived in our village, others were not trustworthy. Since we could not always identify which individuals were dangerous and which were not, similar to our inability to distinguish which nearby snakes were poisonous, we had to view all Whites as a threat until proven otherwise. One mistake could cost us our lives. As a result, I was told never to trust any White person. It is unfortunate, but this was a survival tactic at the time. This was not merely unfounded paranoia; there were events happening around us that made such possibilities seem all too real. When I was 12 years old, there was a 14-year-old Black boy named Emmett Till who traveled one summer from his home in Chicago to Mississippi to visit his cousins. Being from up North in Chicago, he may not have been aware of the serious racial dangers facing young Black boys living among the White Supremacists in the southern state of Mississippi. Very soon during his fun vacation with his cousins, he was kidnapped, tortured, and lynched in Mississippi in 1955, after being accused of making eye contact with and offending a White woman. That sad story is featured in a current heart-breaking movie entitled "Till," produced by Whoopi Goldberg and partners.

Also, a few years earlier, in 1951, in Martinsville, Virginia, fifteen minutes' drive from my home, in the famous legal case The Martinsville Seven, a group of seven Black men, ages 18 to 23, were convicted by an all-White jury and executed. So, the prospective danger of my death was a very real consideration to my parents and grandmother; and they used such examples to stoke fear into my mind. I was told not to play with little White girls, not to make eye contact with White adults, and to step aside in buildings and on the roads to give all White people the priority of their passage.

Of course, we Black people did not attend the same schools or churches, nor go to the same movie theaters or eating places. The implied reason was that we Black people were inferior to White people. However, I had a dangerous problem in that I did not feel inferior to anybody in the entire world. My quickness in learning math, history and vocabulary, my ability to remember nearly everything and my inclination and ability to take charge in most situations led me to believe that God had given me special talents that made me equal or better than anyone else, whether Black or

White. But, admittedly, that kind of thinking on my part in that racially toxic environment was very dangerous for me.

Throughout this book, I mention God and people's race many times, and therefore believe that it is important that I expound on both of those topics. First, on the topic of God, I personally don't believe that the Universe is a random creation; yet, others might rightfully think otherwise. Having studied that topic for four years as a Philosophy Minor at Howard University, I do understand that there is no scientific proof of God's existence, but I personally have chosen to believe it by pure "faith."

What that means is that I don't put pressure on anyone else to believe in God or what is written in the bible. Moreover, I believe, by faith alone, that God is real and gets involved in the actions of mankind, especially when mankind pleads with God to get involved. On the second topic, that of race, I believe that God created all humans to be good and of equal value but that God does not control us like we are puppets. I believe God has granted us "free-will," allowing us to choose to do good or evil. Consequently, some people in every race have decided to do evil, including enslaving other humans. Yes, even some in the Black race have been guilty of capturing and enslaving other Black humans. All enslavement and oppression are evil acts and occur against God's intention. And, from the perspective of a Professor and Philosophy Minor, I view the bible as an outstanding source of wisdom, advice, and role modeling.

Despite facing outrageous racial suppression, challenges, obstacles, and barriers, I managed to perform well in most of the things I was asked to do - whether farm work, academics, or other. But my actions at that time were a mixed bag. In my younger years, I was a very unruly child who stayed in trouble - from constant fights at school, disobeying my teachers and other adults, to breaking into our neighbor Mr. Eddie Strange's store 10 to 20 times until I was finally caught. Looking back, I attribute that bad behavior to being too inquisitive, full of energy and thoughts, and just too gifted in brainpower and anxiety. I was always bursting with energy and wanting to do something. Unfortunately, there was nothing made available to channel my energy into something constructive at that time. Understandably, there was no way that my parents, who were on the farm with 12 children, would have known how to parent an unruly and gifted child. They finally resolved to pray continually for me and hope that the whole village would assist in keeping me alive and out of jail. It worked! It took the entire village to raise the child (me)!

During my youth, no Black child of the thousands who lived in our village, to my knowledge, had earned a college degree. But, with the pleading and inspiration of two of my older sisters, Anne and Thelma, some of my high school teachers, and several elders in my village, I attended college at Howard University in the big city of Washington, DC. At Howard University, I was academically successful, appointed to the highest military cadet rank of Cadet Lt. Colonel of the Air Force, Captain of the Varsity Track team, as well as achieved numerous other awards. After college, I became a Captain in the U.S. Air Force, Chief of the Air Force Computer Data Center at the Pentagon in Virginia, an Executive at General Electric, a Professor at Nyack College-DC Campus, and Founder and President of several small corporations.

In hindsight, it is remarkable that all those wonderful things came to me, in spite of my Black race and poor and disadvantaged country background. I attribute those accomplishments to the powerful encouragement, motivation, and support provided to me by many people of all races and economic and academic levels in many communities as I moved through my life journey. Also, included in the roots of my life success were a lot of Godly blessings, continued personal sacrifices, hard work, and even a little luck.

In recent years, I have spent a lot of time reflecting on how I was able to have such a large, powerful success support team. I think the most important factor was that I always strove to make myself deserving, likable, and communicate appreciativeness to each supporter at all times. There was nothing more important than thanking each supporter face-to-face, over the telephone, via mail, or otherwise for making an investment of their time and other resources toward my success. I spent a lot of time visiting and listening to the wise elders, teachers, coaches, relatives, and others. They knew that I really appreciated all of their support, and they subsequently gave me even more support. Along with that, I knew that I had to make many sacrifices and work very hard to achieve success. For example, I avoided and missed most dances and parties because I wanted to spend extra time on my academic studies and do other things that would contribute to advancing my leadership and performances in various endeavors.

As I've gained knowledge and understanding over the years, I've come to believe that my Blackness and African heritage may have actually worked in my favor. I believe that those of Black African lineage have been granted special access to Supreme Powers or Superpowers by God since the beginning of humankind. These Superpowers are still available to us if we make the necessary sacrifices and do the hard work required to merit and tap into these special God-gifts. My surprising achievements in life were a result of me learning to be humble, reaching out to discern what gifts God may have been offering me, and accepting with expressed gratitude the wisdom and support of my parents, teachers, community Elders, and others. Through this process, I discovered the many Superpowers that God was making available to me and all of us of Black African lineage.

Observing the many top achievements of people of Black African lineage throughout history, in spite of the unbelievable obstacles and barriers they faced, is no longer a surprise to me. A remarkable list of top achievers includes, but is not limited to, Black African academic Universities in Timbuktu and Kemet, Africa, which were the first academic universities in the world; Frederick Douglas, Harriet Tubman, W.E.B. Dubois, Jesse Owens, General Colin Powell, Michael Jordan, President Barack Obama, Katherine Johnson, Muhammad Ali, Thurgood Marshall, Maya Angelou, Simone Biles, Denzel Washington, and Serena Williams, among others. These individuals were operating with unusual powers, more precisely Superpowers.

With this book, I seek to share my personal experience of living under the oppressive racial discrimination of White

Supremacy, fighting off the world's effort to convince me that my Black African race is inferior, and yet finding a way to reach great life success and happiness. My hope is that many Black youth and even some Black adults will learn about the struggles and successes of my life journey and create their own modified version to assist them in achieving their own life success.

My more comprehensive aspiration for them and my grandchildren is the following: First, I hope that they will develop and maintain a high level of ethical and moral integrity, be good people committed to being humble and appreciative of life and other people, and seek to help less fortunate individuals in life. Secondly, I hope they will develop great self-confidence, be strongly driven, highly motivated, and have a spirit of strong determination. The world they face in schools, sports, business, and community is very competitive and will try to intimidate and control them. The seeds of destiny that God has bestowed in them, and the nurturing and training legacy we caring adults are planting in them, should make them resilient against outside oppressive forces.

Thirdly, I want them to learn to sacrifice many of the fun and pleasurable things in life in order to do exceedingly well academically and overall, and to work to gain vast knowledge and wisdom. Success in these areas will position them to be top achievers and great leaders, allowing them to control their own destinies. I offer my journey from childhood to adulthood as just one model they may want to study and use as a template.

INTRODUCTION

As a writer, publisher, speaker, coach, mentor, and successful entrepreneur, I am honored to introduce the book "Black Excellence: Identifying Your God-Given Superpower" by Professor George Hairston. Working on this project has brought me full circle, as I am now a student of the author and publisher of this groundbreaking work. The message of Black Excellence and identifying your God-given superpower has enlightened me in many ways, and I am excited to share this journey with you. I hope this message resonates with you and awakens something inside of you that will provoke action. As you embark on this journey, take a moment to reflect on where you are currently in your life. Then, I want you to imagine where you could be if the possibilities were limitless. Are you ready to embrace the power of Black Excellence? Brace for impact, as this book will challenge you to identify your God-given superpower and unleash it to its full potential.

Black Excellence: Identifying Your God-Given Superpower, is not a book that aims to diminish other races and cultures; it is a book that aims to empower, motivate, and inspire a people who have been made to believe that they are less than. In Chapter One, we take a journey through history that begins in Africa, where God created the first humans, who were Black Africans, and gave them supreme powers to manage the vast universe. Despite the continent's beauty, resourcefulness, and intellectual advancement, the practice of slavery targeted individuals of Black African heritage in the United States, which was the most ruthless, brutal, and sinister form of slavery driven by the racist belief that the Black African race was inferior to the White race. This book aims to help Black and Brown people of color recognize their God-given superpowers and strive for excellence.

Black excellence is a powerful force that has inspired many people to achieve greatness. In "Black Excellence: Identifying Your God-Given Superpower," Professor Hairston celebrates Black Top Achievers of the World who have overcome adversity and achieved remarkable success in their respective fields. These individuals serve as a testament to what can be achieved through hard work, dedication, and belief in oneself. They are examples of the God-given superpowers that exist within the Black community and how they can be harnessed to achieve greatness. By telling our own stories and controlling our narratives, we can overcome the inferiority complex imposed on us by our oppressors. In the second chapter, Professor Hairston explores the various categories of superpowers possessed by Black Top Achievers, including political leadership, medicine, media and entertainment, law and justice, and sports. He also highlights a select list of Black Top Achievers who have excelled in these categories, demonstrating the power of Black excellence and inspiring readers to pursue their own greatness.

Discovering and cultivating your God-given superpower is essential for achieving Black Excellence. As noted in Chapter Three, the keys to top achievers' success are having a strong vision and goal-setting, establishing a supportive network, and applying determination and hard work. However, before embarking on this journey, it's crucial to identify the superpower that fits you best. This is not a one-size-fits-all situation, and it requires deep self-reflection and experimentation. President Obama, for example, tried various things before realizing his true potential in politics. By using tools like the Johari Window and SWOT chart and seeking feedback from your support network, you can hone in on your unique abilities and excel in a field that aligns with your passion and core values. So, let's get ready to access our superpowers and reach new heights of excellence!

In addition to distractions, there is another enemy working against us - those who seek to control our minds. The marketing industry spends billions of dollars each year studying how to influence our decision-making processes and behaviors, often through the use of subliminal messaging and psychological manipulation. This "marketing war" is designed to make us feel inadequate, insecure, and dependent on certain products or services, leading us down a path of consumerism and materialism. It's important to recognize these tactics and be mindful of the messages we're receiving. By doing so, we can avoid becoming modern-day slaves, psychological slaves who are controlled by external forces rather than our own internal values and beliefs. In Chapter Four, we dive deeper into the ways in which our enemies are working to block us from accessing and using our superpowers, and offer strategies to combat these obstacles.

In Chapter Five of Black Excellence: Identifying Your God-Given Superpower, Professor Hairston shares his wisdom blocks, lessons he learned on his journey to achieving Black Excellence. These "wisdom blocks" are universal and serve as reflection points to provide motivation when needed. They are the key to success, and incorporating them into your development is critical. The wisdom blocks range from returning favors, visiting the elderly, looking at opportunities both strategically and tactically, consciously managing career dreams, and turning setbacks into comebacks or opportunities. Professor Hairston's personal experiences, like climbing a 15-foot ladder at 79 and breaking his foot, serve as reminders that setbacks can be turned into opportunities, and the key is to always look for ways to turn them around. This chapter is full of valuable insights and advice from around the world that will help you achieve your potential greatness.

Black Excellence: Identifying Your God-Given Superpower is a book that encourages readers to recognize their potential and tap into their inner strengths to achieve greatness. However, as the author, Professor Hairston, notes in the Call to Action section, the struggle for equal rights, opportunities, and justice for Black Americans is far from over. Despite significant landmarks like the Emancipation Proclamation and the Civil Rights Act, the progress towards equality has been slow and insufficient. In fact, White Supremacist counter-moves have often resulted in setbacks, such as the Jim Crow policies and laws that took away new freedoms from Black people after the Emancipation Proclamation.

While some have lost hope and even moved to foreign countries, new warriors continue to join the battle to keep hope alive. The struggle for equal rights, opportunities, and justice has seen many fighters, including Dr. Martin Luther King Jr., Fannie Lou Hamer, Barbara Jordan, John Lewis, Medgar Evers, Rev. Al Sharpton, Stacey Abrams, James Clyburn, and Rev. Raphael Warnock, among others. However, as Professor Hairston emphasizes, the work is far from complete, and we must remain vigilant.

One significant challenge that the Black community faces is the lack of participation from both Blacks and Whites who choose not to be activists or vote in federal, state, or local elections. With Whites comprising 76% and Blacks only 14% of the U.S. population, we need every vote we can get. However, if we can convince or incentivize 90% of Black and Brown voters to vote, we will have enough votes to pass the Voting Rights bills and equal justice and opportunities bills that are needed.

Professor Hairston draws inspiration from the red ants in the deserts of Phoenix, Arizona, and Scandinavia, which, individually, were not optimistic about building a tall ant hill. However, they were willing to contribute to building a smaller ant hill. Similarly, many Blacks don't believe they have any power and that it is not worth voting. The author calls on Black people to identify with the red ants and join forces to build a 9-foot-high hill of Black voting power. This includes recruiting every young voting-age Black person, every incarcerated Black person, every Black homeless person, and so on, to join the fight for equality.

In conclusion, Black Excellence: Identifying Your God-Given Superpower is a powerful book that recognizes the challenges that Black people have faced in America and encourages readers to tap into their potential and inner strengths to achieve greatness. The Call to Action section urges Black people to pay it forward and help others achieve their highest level of greatness while continuing to fight for equal rights, opportunities, and justice. It is critical to remain vigilant, recruit every young voting-age Black person, and incentivize Blacks and Browns to vote in federal, state, or local elections. Let us join forces and build a 9-foot-high hill of Black voting power to promote equality for all Americans.

Have you ever wondered what makes successful people stand out? What is it that gives them that "extra something" that seems to propel them forward in life? In Black Excellence: Identifying Your God-Given Superpower, you'll discover the key to unlocking your own greatness. Working alongside Professor Hairston, I have gained invaluable insights into the power of knowing who you are and surrounding yourself with people who believe in you. This book isn't just another story - it's a life guide that draws upon Godly principles, personal experiences, and hard-earned knowledge to help you achieve your own path to greatness. As a product of this transformative approach, I can attest that the pages within will inspire, motivate, and educate you on how to unleash your own God-given superpower.

Tamika "TJ" Woodard,
CEO of Quantum Leap Media Group

CONTENTS

Foreword v
Preface ix
Introduction xxi

Chapter 1: God's Special Land and People: Africa and Black Americans 1

Chapter 2: Black Top Achievers of the World Who Took Advantage of God-given Superpowers 6

Chapter 3: How to Achieve Black Excellence in Your Chosen Career Field 27

Chapter 4: Enemies and Various Powers are Working to Block Us from Accessing and Using Our Superpowers 50

Chapter 5: "Wisdom Blocks" From Around the World to Help You Achieve Your Potential Greatness 61

Chapter 6: Urgent Call to Action: We Must Continue the Fight for Equal Rights, Opportunities and Justice for Black Americans! 76

Acknowledgements	81
Our Recommended Sources of Facts, Knowledge, Wisdom and Advice	83
About The Author	95
References	99

CHAPTER 1
GOD'S SPECIAL LAND AND PEOPLE: AFRICA AND BLACK AMERICANS

> *"God chose Africa to be the first home for the first humans He created, and God gave those Black humans Supreme Powers to be able to manage the Universe."*

Ancient Black Africa

The Book of Genesis in the Holy Bible states that God created everything, including the oceans, land, mountains, forests, the sun, the moon, and all living creatures. Feeling lonely, God created the first two humans, who were Black Africans, and placed them in the Garden of Eden, located in Botswana, Africa. These first humans were God's "chosen people" and were given access to supreme powers to manage the vast universe. However, God did not create humans as puppets and allowed them to exercise their free will. Over time, humans evolved into different colors, sizes, and shapes. Sadly, throughout history, many people and groups have committed evil acts, often driven by financial gain. Enslavement of others is one of the worst evils committed by humans. The practice of slavery was prevalent in the Roman Empire, but it was not based on skin color. The Apartheid policy in South Africa enforced a caste system based solely on skin color, but it was not comprehensive slavery. However, the United States of America had the most ruthless, brutal, and sinister form of slavery, which targeted individuals of Black African heritage. This policy was driven by the racist belief that the Black African race was inferior to the White race and made good economic sense for the growth of the American economy. This racist view was prevalent among White European nations, as demonstrated by the Berlin Conference. The conference included several nations that divided up the African continent as colonies. King Leopold II of Belgium, for example, took the Congo and brutally slaughtered ten million Black people. Despite these atrocities, the African continent remains beautiful and rich in resources.

Africa, "God's Chosen Land"

The continent now known as Africa, which was once beautiful, resource-rich, and intellectually advanced, has had several names, including Alkebulan (meaning "The Garden of Eden" or "Mother of Mankind"), Nubia, and Kemet. In ancient times, Africa was a thriving land of business, trade, and academic and scientific advancement, surpassing European nations and the rest of the world. The Nubian civilization is considered the "cradle of civilization" and is believed to date back more than 17,000 years. Despite what some people may believe, the oldest academic universities in the world were located in Africa, specifically in the countries of Egypt, Morocco, and Mali. The most well-known of these were the libraries of Kemet and the Temples at Timbuktu. Psalms 68:31 speaks of God's love for Africa and its people, and His promise that princes, kings, and queens will come out of Egypt (Africa), and Ethiopia will soon stretch out her hands unto God. Africa, which is the world's second-largest continent, is also the richest in gold, diamonds, and other natural resources, and comprises 54 countries, including Egypt, Ethiopia, Kenya, Ghana, Nigeria, and Timbuktu.

Egypt, known for its majestic pyramids, Great Sphinx, Luxor's hieroglyph-lined Karnak Temple, Valley of the Kings tombs, and the 25th Pharaoh Dynasty, is renowned for its Black African marvels that are unrivaled. Ethiopia is a country with a rich Black African culture, with archaeological findings dating back over 3 million years. Among the significant sites is Lalibela, featuring rock-cut Christian churches from the 12th-13th centuries. The most distinguished leader of Ethiopia was a Black African referred to as "His Imperial Highness Emperor Haile Selassie," who is said to be a traceable cousin of Jesus Christ.

Africa Today

Africa is a continent of immense beauty and resources. Kenya, with its capital city Nairobi, is home to 54 million people and boasts 50 stunning parks and reserves. The first Black African woman to win the Nobel Peace Prize was Wangari Muta Maathai from Kenya. President Barack Obama, a Black African man of Kenyan heritage, was also a Nobel Peace Prize winner. Ghana, with a population of 31 million people, is experiencing an economic boom thanks to gold, cocoa, and oil. It was a significant trading center in the 13th century. However, China's billions of dollars of investment are putting Ghana under its control. Nigeria, with a population of 213 million people, is the world's most populous Black nation and the hub for Africa's fashion, technology, and creativity. The second-largest film industry globally is located in Nigeria. I've only highlighted five of the 54 African countries, and each has its fantastic history.

This has caused China and the U.S. to compete fiercely to gain an edge in their dealings with Africa. They are vying for full ownership and business trading positions on the continent. In late

2022, President Joe Biden held a U.S.-African Leaders Summit in Washington, D.C., which was attended by 49 of the 54 African countries. The summit concluded with the President pledging $55 billion to support the African countries economically, vastly improving the U.S.'s relationship with Africa after the previous U.S. President characterized Black/African countries as "shit-hole countries." Despite this, most White European countries and people still view people with Black African lineage as inferior to them.

It's important to note that the real Africa is not the version portrayed in White Supremacist photos and movies depicting vast wilderness, savage animals, and naked people running around in the jungle, where White Tarzan communicates with and manages the beasts. The White Supremacists promote the idea that a White man like Tarzan is brilliant enough to communicate with animals, while the inferior race, Black Africans, live among those same animals but are not intelligent enough to communicate with them. We must write our own stories and control our narratives; otherwise, the oppressors will lead us to develop a strong inferiority complex. It is up to each Black individual to tell their story, research their own history of Black excellence, and educate our Black African race, particularly our youth, about these facts.

CHAPTER 2
BLACK TOP ACHIEVERS OF THE WORLD WHO TOOK ADVANTAGE OF GOD-GIVEN SUPERPOWERS.

> "Until the lion (Black people) learns to write, every story about the hunt will glorify the hunter (the oppressor of Black people)" — An African Igbo Proverb

> "If you are not careful, the newspapers (and Mass Media) will have you hating the people who are being oppressed and loving the people who are doing the oppressing"
> — Malcom X

Africa is a continent of immense beauty and resources. Kenya, with its capital city Nairobi, is home to 54 million people and boasts 50 stunning parks and reserves. The first Black African woman to win the Nobel Peace Prize was Wangari Muta Maathai from Kenya. President Barack Obama, a Black African man of Kenyan heritage, was also a Nobel Peace Prize winner. Ghana, with a population of 31 million people, is experiencing an economic boom thanks to gold, cocoa, and oil. It was a significant trading center in the 13th century. However, China's billions of dollars of investment are putting Ghana under its control. Nigeria, with a population of 213 million people, is the world's most populous Black nation and the hub for Africa's fashion, technology, and creativity. The second-largest film industry globally is located in Nigeria. I've only highlighted five of the 54 African countries, and each has its fantastic history.

This has caused China and the U.S. to compete fiercely to gain an edge in their dealings with Africa. They are vying for full ownership and business trading positions on the continent. In late 2022, President Joe Biden held a U.S.-African Leaders Summit in Washington, D.C., which was attended by 49 of the 54 African countries. The summit concluded with the President pledging $55 billion to support the African countries economically, vastly improving the U.S.'s relationship with Africa after the previous U.S. President characterized Black/African countries as "shit-hole countries." Despite this, most White European countries and people still view people with Black African lineage as inferior to them.

It's important to note that the real Africa is not the version portrayed in White Supremacist photos and movies depicting vast wilderness, savage animals, and naked people running around in the jungle, where White Tarzan communicates with and manages the beasts. The White Supremacists promote the idea that a White man like Tarzan is brilliant enough to communicate with animals, while the inferior race, Black Africans, live among those same animals but are not intelligent enough to communicate with them. We must write our own stories and control our narratives; otherwise, the oppressors will lead us to develop a strong inferiority complex. It is up to each Black individual to tell their story, research their own history of Black excellence, and educate our Black African race, particularly our youth, about these facts.

Furthermore, it's worth noting that despite the racist barriers and obstacles placed in their way, Black Top Achievers succeeded greatly in their respective fields. My belief is that their success is attributable to a unique set of Superpowers bestowed upon Black people by God during the creation of the Universe. These Superpowers are supernatural and superhuman abilities and attributes that certain individuals possess and utilize in their activities or performances. We can see the manifestation of these Superpowers in the remarkable achievements of Black Top Achievers in various areas of life, such as knowledge, academics, artistic performance, athletic performance, leadership, and many others. It's essential to point out that not all the categories of Superpowers and the Black Top Achievers who utilized them are fully documented in history books. However, some of the categories and a selective list of Black Top Achievers who excelled in those categories are as follows:

Political Leadership: President Barack Obama, President of the United States of America; Rep. John Lewis, Distinguished Member of the U.S. House of Representatives; Stacey Abrams, Outstanding Political Leader in the State of Georgia; Rep. James Clyburn, Distinguished Member of the U.S. House of Representatives.

Medical Doctors: Dr. Charles Drew, Dr. Patricia Era Bath, Dr. Daniel Williams, Dr. Ben Carson, and Dr. Marilyn Hughes Gaston

Media Entertainment: Sammy Davis, Jr., Dancer, Singer, and Movie Star; Oprah Winfrey, TV and Media Mogul; Tyler Perry, Movie Producer and Philanthropist; and Actors Sydney Poitier, Denzel Washington, Chadwick Boseman

Law and Justice: Justice Thurgood Marshall, Former Justice of the U.S. Supreme Court; Eric Holder, Former U.S. Attorney

General; Ketanji Brown-Jackson, Justice of the U.S. Supreme Court

Sports: Basketball: Wilt Chamberlain, Michael Jordan, Kobe Bryant, Magic Johnson and LeBron James

Baseball: Satchel Paige, Jackie Robinson, Willie Mays, Hank Aron, Roberto Clemente

Football: Jim Brown, Barry Sanders, Patrick Mahone, Warren Moon, Jalen Hurts

Other Sports: Althea Gibson, Arthur Ashe, and Serena and Venus Williams in tennis; Tiger Woods in golf; Simone Biles in gymnastics; and Pele and Kylian Mbappe in soccer

Science/Inventors: George Washington Carver, Mae Jemison, Shirley Jackson, Ernest Just, Katherine Johnson

Poets and Writers: Phyllis Wheatley, Langston Hughes, Maya Angelou, Zora Neale Hurston, and Amanda Gorman

Singers: Mahalia Jackson, Billie Holiday, Nina Simone, Marvin Gaye, Aretha Franklin, and Whitney Houston

Religious Leaders: Rev. Dr. Martin Luther King, Jr., Rev. Dr. Jeremiah Wright, Minister Malcolm X, and Rev. Al Sharpton,

Homeless People Who Yet Became Top Achievers: Sydney Poitier, Halle Berry, and Tyler Perry

A More In-depth Look at a Few Super-outstanding Black Top Achievers

Shaka Zulu, a Genius Military Leader of Africa

The Zulu state in Africa was formed by Shaka Zulu, who ruled as the King from 1816 to 1828. Shaka was the stuff of legends, and subsequent tales of his life include a prophecy foretold of a child that would make the Zulu the most feared of nations. Shaka's success was due to his spectacular improvements to the traditional weapons (spear, club, and shield) and new battle strategies. As a result, Zulu military regiments could cover up to 50 miles (80 kilometers) a day and still be able to fight a battle at the end of the march. In comparison, European armies of the day could barely cover 20 miles (32 kilometers) in a day and rarely were able to engage an enemy at the end of a day's march.

Phyllis Wheatley, Acclaimed Poet, and Publisher

Phyllis Wheatley was the first Black person, male or female, to write and publish a book of poems in the United States of America. She was born in Senegal, Africa, and was sold as a slave at the age of seven to the Wheatley family in Boston, Massachusetts. She wrote poems in English when she was just 13 years old. When she was 21, she was taken to court to prove that she was the author of her own poems, as Black people were widely believed to be inferior and incapable of writing poetry and books.

Thurgood Marshall, Associate Justice of the U.S. Supreme Court

Justice Thurgood Marshall, a prominent American civil rights lawyer and jurist, made history by serving as the first Black Justice of the United States Supreme Court from 1967 to 1991. He is best known for his monumental victory in the landmark "Brown v. Board of Education" case, which declared the unconstitutional nature of the "Separate but Equal" policy that was previously in place.

Muhammad Ali, The Greatest Heavyweight Boxer of All Time

Muhammad Ali, in his own words, once said, "I'm not the greatest. I'm the double greatest. Not only do I knock 'em out, I pick the round. I'm the boldest, the prettiest, the most superior, most scientific, most skillful boxer in the ring. I'm the onliest fighter who goes from street corner to street corner and club to club debating with fans. I've received more publicity than any other fighter in history. I talk to reporters till their fingers are sore." Through his boxing career, Ali became an internationally recognized advocate for equality and justice for all people, regardless of race.

Rev. Dr. Martin Luther King, Jr., World Spiritual, and Social Justice Leader

Dr. King, the son of an earlier civil rights activist and minister Rev. Martin Luther King, Sr., was an American Baptist minister and social justice activist. He was one of the most prominent leaders in the Civil Rights Movement from 1955 until his assassination in 1968. Inspired by the beliefs of the nonviolent activism of Mahatma Gandhi of India, the young Dr. King advanced civil rights for Black and all other people in the United States through a program and philosophy of nonviolence and civil disobedience. He led targeted, nonviolent resistance against the vicious Jim Crow laws and other forms of discrimination against Black people.

Harriet Tubman, Slave Abolitionist, Suffrage Leader, and Slavery Freedom Fighter

Known as the "Moses of her people," Harriet Tubman was formerly enslaved, then escaped and helped others gain their freedom as a "conductor" of the Underground Railroad. Tubman also served as a scout, spy, guerrilla soldier, and nurse for the Union Army during the Civil War.

Hannibal the Great, a Highly Educated Black Russian Military General

Hannibal Barca was actually born in 247 BC in Carthage, which is modern-day Tunisia in North Africa. He was a Carthaginian general and is considered one of the greatest military tacticians and strategists in history. Hannibal is known for his victories in the Second Punic War, particularly his crossing of the Alps with his army and elephants.

Nelson Mandella, Former President of South Africa

Nelson Rolihlahla Mandela was a South African anti-apartheid activist who served as the first President of South Africa from 1994 to 1999. He was the country's first Black head of state and the first elected in a fully representative democratic election in South Africa.

President Barack Obama, 44th President of the United States of America

President Barack Obama was the 44th President of the United States from 2009 to 2017. As a member of the Democratic Party, Obama was the first Black President of the United States, surprising the world by serving two terms.

Frederick Douglas, Abolitionist, Orator, Writer, and Social Reformer

Frederick Douglass, known as "the Great Emancipator," was a formerly enslaved man who became a prominent emancipation activist, author, and public speaker. He became a leader in the abolitionist movement, which sought to end the practice of slavery before and during the Civil War.

Dr. George Washington Carver, American Agricultural Scientist, and Inventor

Dr. George Washington Carver, a pioneering agricultural scientist, is renowned for his incredible achievements in creating more than 500 innovative products from peanuts and sweet potatoes. Some of the products he developed include milk, cooking oils, paper, wood stains, soap, and cosmetics. His groundbreaking work continues to inspire many to this day, and his legacy serves as a testament to his unwavering dedication to scientific research and improving the world around him.

Madam C. J. Walker, Black Business Founder, and Political and Social Activist

Madam C. J. Walker, a pioneering Black business entrepreneur, philanthropist, and political and social activist, was born in 1867 in Irvington, New York. She gained worldwide recognition for her exceptional achievements, including being recorded as the first female self-made millionaire in America in the Guinness Book of World Records. Madam Walker was a specialist in making hair care products, which she developed to cater to the needs of Black women. Her contributions to the beauty industry have left a lasting impact, and her legacy continues to inspire many to this day.

LeBron James, Philanthropist, One of the Greatest Basketball Players of All Times

LeBron James has been a basketball prodigy since elementary school, despite growing up in the inner-city where he experienced poverty, street violence, and the struggles of being raised in a single-parent household. Despite the challenges he faced, he has built an incredible career and amassed a fortune of over $1 billion through various contracts and endorsements. He is committed to giving back to his community and has donated more than $100 million to organizations supporting basic amenities, education, and quality housing. This includes opening his own school and granting scholarships to support education. Despite not having a father or a college education, LeBron was signed for $420,000 per year when he was just 18 years old. He has since become one of the highest-paid athletes in the world, earning around $2 million per week. LeBron's generosity extends beyond financial donations as he has sent over 1000 children to college with fully paid tuition, providing them with opportunities he didn't have growing up.

Mae C. Jemison, Engineer, Medical Physician, and Former NASA Astronaut

Born in Decatur, Alabama in 1956, Ms. Jemison is a pioneering figure in the fields of science and space exploration. She obtained a medical degree from Weill Medical College in 1981 and an engineering degree from Stanford University in 1977, showcasing her interdisciplinary talents. Ms. Jemison made history in 1992 when she became the first Black woman to travel into space, serving as a mission specialist aboard the Space Shuttle Endeavour in the U.S. Space Program. Her remarkable achievements have paved the way for many women and people of color who aspire to pursue careers in science and space exploration.

Marian Rogers Croak, an Outstanding Scientist

Marian Rogers Croak is a highly accomplished engineer who currently serves as the Vice President of Engineering at Google. Prior to her tenure at Google, she was the Senior Vice President of Research and Development at AT&T, where she made significant contributions to the field of telecommunications. With over 200 patents to her name, she is widely recognized as a pioneering inventor and innovator. Her outstanding achievements were honored in 2013 when she was inducted into the Women in Technology International Hall of Fame. Among her many contributions, her invention that allows users to make calls over the internet instead of a phone line has revolutionized the telecommunications industry. Her work has had a profound impact on the world and has inspired countless individuals to pursue careers in science and technology.

Benjamin Banneker, Inventor, Astronomer, and Mathematician

Benjamin Banneker was a remarkable figure in American history, born to a slave father and a mother who had been freed from slavery. He achieved great success as a mathematician, astronomer, and surveyor. He gained recognition for his work when he published an almanac featuring astronomical and water tide calculations between 1791 and 1802. This publication was a significant achievement in a time when African Americans had limited opportunities for education and career advancement. His talents caught the attention of President Thomas Jefferson, who recommended Banneker for a position as a surveyor in the original borders of the District of Columbia. Despite facing discrimination and prejudice, Banneker persevered, and his contributions to science and society continue to inspire people today.

Langston Hughes, Famous Black Poet Political and Social Justice Activist

Langston Hughes was an influential American writer and poet who played a significant role in the Harlem Renaissance. Through his writing, he brought the Black American experience to the forefront and used his art to promote social justice and equality. His diverse body of work included poetry, plays, novels, and newspaper columns, all of which showcased his unique style and talent. Over his career, he wrote more than 400 poems that continue to inspire and influence poets today. His contributions to American literature and the Civil Rights movement remain an enduring legacy of his powerful voice and vision.

Katherine Johnson, Phenomenal Mathematician, First "Human Computer"

Katherine Johnson, a remarkable woman born in West Virginia in 1918, achieved extraordinary things in her lifetime. Despite the challenges she faced as a woman and a minority, Katherine excelled academically, graduating from high school at just 14 and college at 18. She went on to work for NASA, where she used her expertise in mathematics to calculate the paths for spacecraft to orbit Earth and land on the Moon. Her calculations were critical to NASA's success, and her work played a vital role in sending astronauts into orbit and later to the Moon and back. Katherine's incredible achievements and contributions to space exploration have inspired generations of young people to pursue careers in science and technology.

Ava DuVernay, Distinguished Hollywood Filmmaker and Director

Ava Marie DuVernay is a highly accomplished film producer born in California in 1972. Her impressive body of work has earned her hundreds of awards over the years, but one of her most noteworthy achievements was her work on Selma, a biopic about the life of Dr. Martin Luther King, Jr. Her outstanding contribution to the film earned her the distinction of being the first Black woman to be nominated for a Golden Globe Award for Best Director and the Academy Award for Best Picture. Furthermore, Ms. DuVernay became the first Black woman to direct a film with a budget exceeding $100 million. In recognition of her significant accomplishments, she was featured on Time magazine's list of the 100 most influential people in the world in 2017.

Tiger Woods, World Famous Professional Golfer

Eldrick "Tiger" Woods is a world-renowned American professional golfer. With a remarkable record of PGA Tour wins, he shares the top spot with another golfer. Additionally, he ranks second in men's major championships and holds several other golfing records. Woods' extraordinary talent on the golf course has earned him the distinction of being considered one of the greatest golfers ever, and his name is synonymous with the sport. Moreover, he is widely recognized as one of the most famous athletes in modern history, having captured the hearts of fans worldwide with his impressive performances on the course.

Ketanji Brown-Jackson, Associate Justice of the Supreme Court of the United States

Born in Washington, DC in 1970 and raised in Miami, Florida, Justice Brown-Jackson is an accomplished legal professional. She attended Harvard University for both her undergraduate studies and law school, where she earned the distinction of serving as the Harvard Law Review editor. In June 2022, Justice Brown-Jackson made history by succeeding U.S. Supreme Court Justice Breyer, becoming the first Black woman to serve on the United States Supreme Court. Her appointment is a testament to her remarkable achievements and a significant milestone for diversity and representation in the legal profession.

Oprah Winfrey, Billionaire Multimedia Network Host

Oprah Gail Winfrey, or simply Oprah, was born in 1954 in Mississippi and is a highly successful American personality. She wears many hats, including those of a talk show host, television producer, actress, author, and philanthropist. Oprah is most famous for her talk show, The Oprah Winfrey Show, which was broadcast from Chicago and ran in national syndication for an impressive 25 years, from 1986 to 2011. She has amassed a net worth of over $2.5 billion, making her one of the wealthiest women in the world. Despite her wealth and success, Oprah is known for her generosity and philanthropic efforts, which have made a positive impact on many people's lives.

Nasara James Dabo

Nasara is a 13-year-old girl from Nigeria with an extraordinary talent for mathematics. In 2022, she achieved a remarkable feat by solving 34 math questions in just 172 seconds to win the gold medal at the International Mathematical Olympiad Competition. Her outstanding achievement is a testament to her hard work, dedication, and exceptional intelligence. Nasara's achievement is even more impressive because she is a Black African, breaking down stereotypes and shattering barriers. Her accomplishment is indeed magical and a source of inspiration for young people around the world.

David Balogun, Black African Student Genius

David Balogun, is a 9-year-old Nigerian American who recently accomplished an incredible feat by graduating from high school in Pennsylvania. He was even awarded the 2022 Distinguished Student Award by the Pennsylvania Association of Gifted Education. In an interview with FOX43, David credited his success to his hard work, his parents, and the Reach Cyber Charter School. He also expressed his realization that he could achieve great things as long as he put in the effort. David's extraordinary accomplishment showcases the immense potential and intelligence that exists within the Black community, and serves as an inspiration to us all.

I must admit that while compiling this list of Black Top Achievers, I have left out countless others who have excelled in various fields. Just imagine how many more Black people could have become Top Achievers if they were not oppressed by the world, facing barriers and obstacles. It would take numerous books to recognize all their accomplishments properly. Nevertheless, this short list clearly demonstrates that our Black African heritage does not lead to inferior achievements in any way. In fact, it may indicate the opposite - that our lineage grants us access to Superpowers that enable us to achieve superior results. Therefore, we may be exceptional in achieving great things. Regarding achieving excellence, we can gain some wisdom from Aristotle, the famous White European Greek Philosopher, who Black teachers educated at the Black Universities in Kemet/Timbuktu.

In the next chapter, I will provide some recommendations to help those interested in achieving their Black excellence.

CHAPTER 3
HOW TO ACHIEVE BLACK EXCELLENCE IN YOUR CHOSEN CAREER FIELD.

> *"Excellence is never an accident. It is always the result of high intention, sincere effort, and intelligent execution."*
> *~ Aristotle*

Life provides us with major opportunities and challenges. You Can Surely become successful, if you use All Resources That Are Available to You. But, Also Know That there are enemies among us who want to suppress and defeat us.

However, with God's backing, we are solely able to achieve our potential destinies of success. So, let's make it happen!

The Secrets to Top Achievers Successes

Let's make one thing clear: not everyone desires to be a star, a top achiever, or a top performer. Some argue that the high expectations and pressure of stardom can lead to addiction and early deaths, as seen with Billie Holiday, Michael Jackson, and Whitney Houston.

However, there are thousands of top achievers who have managed to avoid such tragedies. The difference in outcome may depend on whether a top achiever can maintain a strong sense of self and not let their achievement overshadow their core values.

It's essential to remember that what we do for a living doesn't define who we are as individuals. As unique human beings, our race and career choice should not limit our potential for greatness. Whitney Houston, for instance, had a beautiful voice and sang in her mother's church choir as a teenager. However, her talent led her down a path that didn't align with her core self. She never had the chance to define who she was or separate her excellent singing ability from her identity. As a result, when her career turned negative, she felt like a failure and developed a negative self-image that eventually led to addiction and her untimely death.

It's crucial to make a conscious effort to define and understand who we are as individuals, separate from our circumstances and career choices. For example, President Barack Obama had a challenging childhood. As a young Black man with a Kenyan father who he saw only twice, raised by his grandparents in a White-dominated society in Hawaii, he faced many obstacles. But, with the help of an exceptional support network, he managed to move forward and become the 44th President of the United States.

Another recent example is Andrea Joy Campbell, a young Black woman who became the Attorney General of Massachusetts in January 2023. Despite losing both of her parents at a young age and growing up in low-income housing, she developed a vision for success and, with the help of a strong support network, achieved a Bachelor of Arts degree from Princeton University and a Law degree from the University of California Los Angeles (UCLA).

In both cases, the ultimate successes can be attributed to a common thread: a strong vision and goal-setting, a supportive network, and determination and hard work. It's these qualities that can lead anyone to become a top achiever and enjoy a life of success and happiness.

Your Ultimate Success is Literally in Your Mind and Hands

It is crucial to understand and believe that anyone can become a top achiever. When we are born, we come into the world as a blank slate, with no innate ideas or beliefs. Our parents, early caregivers, and environment begin the process of shaping us. As we grow older, what we read, hear, watch, and believe also contribute to our molding. I call this ongoing process "molding," and the good news is that we can re-mold or reprogram ourselves throughout our lives.

In our early teens, we can start to take responsibility for molding ourselves into successful top achievers by drawing upon extensive outside resources. Here are some steps that can help us reach our goals:

The keys to success are like a three-legged stool: <u>Strong Vision and Goal-Setting</u>, <u>Establishing and Maintaining a Strong Support Network</u>, and <u>Applying Your Own Determination and Hard Work.</u> By combining these three elements, we can become top achievers and enjoy a life of great success and happiness.

Discovering Yourself and Establishing a Vision and Goals: Getting Ready to Access Your Superpowers!

> *"Get the Vision, Write it Down!"* --- Holy Bible, Habakkuk 2:2-3

Not everyone is blessed with the same superpower gift. It's not like browsing through a shopping catalogue and selecting a career or superpower that will make the most money or be the most attractive. Instead, we need to identify the gift that is the best fit for us. We should not envy someone else's gift, but find one that brings us joy and satisfaction while allowing us to perform at a high level. For example, having a musical superpower may not qualify someone to become a U.S. Supreme Court Justice. Likewise, possessing the gymnastics superpower may not allow someone to compete effectively in basketball against LeBron James. It's important to experiment with different things and find one's niche, something they love to do and are good at. President Obama did a lot of soul-searching and experimentation before finding his calling in the world of politics. He pursued his interest in social justice in high school, college, and law school before realizing his true potential.

To find one's best match in a superpower, it's important to get to know oneself through different tools and seek input and assistance from one's support network. In school, one can try out a variety of things such as art, music, designing a computer app, writing articles for the school newspaper, joining a Toastmaster public speaking club, or trying out for a sports team. Keeping track of which activities one likes best and is good at can help in the process of finding a suitable superpower. Additionally, using tools such as **the Johari Window** and a **SWOT chart**, which depict _strengths_, _weaknesses_, _opportunities_, and _threats_, can help structure and formalize the process of finding a suitable superpower.

Johari Window

From Wikipedia, the free encyclopedia

Johari Window

	Known to self	Not known to self
Known to others	Arena	Blind Spot
Not Known to Others	Façade	Unknown

The Johari window is a useful tool designed to help people understand their relationship with themselves and others. Created in 1955 by psychologists Joseph Luft and Harrington Ingham, the technique is commonly used in self-help and corporate settings. The name "Johari" comes from a combination of the founders' first names. The concept is sometimes referred to as the Johari House and has four rooms: Room one contains the parts of ourselves that we and others see, Room two includes aspects of ourselves that others see but we are unaware of, Room three is our private space that we know but hide from others, and Room four is the unconscious part of us that neither ourselves nor others see.

Another useful tool for personal and organizational success planning is the SWOT analysis. This basic tool examines positive and negative factors from an internal and external perspective. It can be used to evaluate and plan for a person, project, or organization, with tailored outcomes for each subject.

- **Strengths(S):** What do you do well? What advantage do you have over others?
- **Weaknesses(W):** What are your shortcomings? Where do other people have an advantage over you?
- **Opportunities(O):** How can you exploit your advantages to succeed?
- **Threats(T):** What could work to block you from your success?

SWOT Analysis Templates — HubSpot

SWOT analysis for:

Strengths	Weaknesses
1.	1.
2.	2.
3.	3.
4.	4.
5.	5.

Opportunities	Threats
1.	1.
2.	2.
3.	3.
4.	4.
5.	5.

How do you write a good SWOT analysis?

When conducting a strategic SWOT analysis of yourself, there are several steps you'll want to take. Here's a breakdown:

1. **Find a free and editable SWOT Analysis Template**, or create your own if you prefer.

2. **Arrange each section into a table with four quadrants.** This visual aid can help you better understand your analysis.
3. **Identify your objective.** Be specific with what you want to analyze.
4. **Identify your strengths.** What are you currently doing well? What factors are in your favor? What do you offer that your competitors can't beat?
5. **Identify your weaknesses.** What roadblocks are hindering you from reaching your goals? What do your competitors offer that continue to be a thorn in your side?
6. **Consider your opportunities.** Dream big and think about potential opportunities that could happen. Include them in your SWOT analysis.
7. **Think about potential threats.** Write down your threats to evaluate them objectively. Divide and conquer them by listing them in terms of least and most likely to occur. This will help you prepare for potential obstacles that could decrease your chances of success.

Below are two examples of a **SWOT Analysis** created by Professor Hairston that can be used.

SWOT Analysis

- Hemingway <u>Team</u>
- Personal _____

Strengths (S)

Top Skills

1. _____
2. _____
3. _____

Like Most

1. _____
2. _____
3. _____

Weaknesses (W)

Top Weaknesses

1. _____
2. _____
3. _____

Dislike Most

1. _____
2. _____
3. _____

Threats (T)

1. _____
2. _____
3. _____

Opportunities (O)

1. _____
2. _____
3. _____

Copyright: Prof. George C. Hairston

Success Warriors, Inc.
"Committed to Our Children... the Future."

(A 501 (c) 3 Non-profit Organization)
www.successwarriors.org
(Cell): 301-520-1074

Leading the Charge to Make Our Youth Successful:

Youth Success Plan For: _____   _____

Date

VISION-BUILDING:

Your Life Purposes (What you hope to become):

Career Goal #1: _____

Career Goal #2: _____

Career Goal #3: _____

Your Mentors:

    #1: _____

    #2: _____

    #3: _____

Education Required for Your Career Goals:

Career #1: _____

Career #2: _____

Career #3: _____

Want to Go to College? If so, what are your top choices?

Special Alert: Goal-setting Should Never be Considered to be Complete:

LeBron James recently shared his goal-setting strategy with ESPN, saying, "It's still mind-boggling to myself. I've set out goals throughout my whole career -- I wanted to be Rookie of the Year, MVP in this league, win championships, be an All-Star, lead the league in assists, make the All-Defensive team, and be Defensive Player of the Year. I never said I wanted to lead the league in scoring or to be the all-time leader in scoring. That's never been a dream of mine. To sit here and actually be on the brink of it happening, it's pretty crazy." Despite this, he expressed his excitement about the upcoming achievement, viewing records not as personal accomplishments, but as human achievements.

Developing and Maintaining a Strong Support Network

Choosing Between a "Do it Alone" Approach and a "Use All Available Resources" Approach

As we journey through life, we're faced with numerous choices that shape our future. One vital decision is deciding how much we want to rely on ourselves and receive all the credit versus tapping into the knowledge, skills, and support of others and giving them credit and thanks for their contribution.

From a young age, I was fascinated by the concept of success and how it's achieved. As a baseball enthusiast, I observed that no single player could lead their team to a world championship. Building a great team and aligning them towards a common goal was critical to success. I also recognized that I didn't have the financial resources to achieve anything significant alone, and I needed support to realize my ambitions.

I looked around my community and noticed that the older adults, known as the Elders, had a wealth of knowledge, understanding, and wisdom that I could learn from. So, I started spending time with them, listening intently to their experiences, and reflecting on their insights. As they saw my commitment, they offered their help and pledged to support me in reaching my dreams of success.

Looking back, I realized how much value and self-worth I gave to the older adults in my community by spending time with them and showing them respect. When someone invests their time and resources in our success, we should reciprocate by doing the same for them.

As an adult, I've made it a game to provide articles, advice, and examples to everyone in my support network, giving back and investing in their happiness and success as they did for me. After all, achieving success isn't a solo endeavor, but rather a team effort.

It's important to be intentional when seeking and using the wisdom of everyone in your support network. Learn from the Top Achievers who have come before you and work to build upon their accomplishments to reach even greater heights. This involves identifying and selecting the best and most appropriate role models to follow. You don't have to be exactly like any one of them, but rather, choose the best features or characteristics from several of them and incorporate them into your own unique self.

When putting together a great support team, remember that your selections don't have to be permanent. As you gain confidence and success, you may want to update or improve your choices. This was the case for my daughter Tanya when she was a teenager. She initially chose Dr. Robert Jones, a successful Black dentist who was a friend of our family, as her role model. Tanya wanted to become a dentist like him and have a big house, pool, and a nice car like he did.

Rather than try to discourage her, my wife and I decided to encourage her dream and help her achieve it. We arranged for her to talk with Dr. Jones to learn what kind of grades she would need to get and what courses she needed to take. Tanya pursued her studies diligently and made those A's and B's. However, she later decided that she wanted to become a lawyer instead of a dentist. By that time, Dr. Jones had become a member of her support team, and Tanya chose a different primary role model, Lawyer Richard Conn, a White lawyer friend of her Uncle Dr. George C. Branche III.

Tanya made herself likeable and appreciative, and Richard became a member of her support team, mentoring her for over 20 years. Tanya ultimately became a Yale Law School graduate and highly successful in the field of law. It's worth noting that Tanya wasn't reluctant to stand on the shoulders of Dr. Branche, Dr. Jones, and Lawyer Conn to achieve her goals.

Here is a recent statement by Joseph Wetteny, an immigrant from Haiti who now lives in the United States. He wants to thank and appreciate his career support team for helping him achieve his success.

Joseph Wetteny says that when he was growing up in Haiti, his parents were always worried about how they were going to feed him and his siblings. But now, he is proud to work with a team that helps to answer the same question for billions of people around the world. Joseph has faced many hardships and learned many lessons on his journey from Haiti to the US, and he believes that his success is due to the many people who have helped him along the way. However, he is most grateful to his earliest mentors, who saw something in him that he couldn't see in himself and gave him the confidence to achieve his goals. Now that he is a manager himself, Joseph is committed to supporting and empowering his team, just as his mentors did for him.

Joseph also has some advice for anyone who wants to build a strong support network. He believes that it's important to be careful and critical when choosing the people who will be on your team. Don't just pick your friends or people who always agree with you. Instead, choose people who are strong enough to disagree with you when necessary and who love you enough to tell you the truth, even if it's not what you want to hear. Joseph has seen firsthand that sometimes people who seem like friends are not really true friends. He once saw a post on social media that said, "I asked God to give me a list of my enemies, and when He did so, I was shocked to see so many of my friend's names on the enemies list."

Joseph has many people in his support network, including Rev. William Hairston of Reidsville, NC, Rev. Dr. Bryon Williams of Maryland, and Calvin Johnson of Atlanta, GA. These people have been with him for a long time, and he values their friendship and support. Joseph's advice to anyone is to never stop working with your network members, because they can help you achieve great things.

Sacrificial Hard Work Required to Become a Top Achiever:

We've all heard the saying, "All work and no play will make Johnny a dull boy!" But I have my own take on it: "All play and no work will make Johnny a failure!" Finding a balance between work and play is important, but I chose to prioritize work and make many sacrifices. I figured that if I worked extra hard in my younger years, I could have more time for leisure activities like vacations, fishing, and golf when I'm older. Some of my sacrifices included limiting my dates to less than 10 during my four years at Howard University and skipping many social parties. I spent a lot of time studying on weekends and molded myself into an avid reader of books on mankind and the world.

I remember making a significant decision after college when I was traveling from Virginia to Nebraska for my role as an Officer in the U.S. Air Force. I spent my last few hundred dollars on a 60-volume set of books called Great Books of the Western World. Those books have stood the test of time and have given me a solid foundation to stand on, especially in history, medicine, philosophy, religion, mathematics, and astronomy. I've since given that set of books to my daughter, Tanya. The decision to read extensively was the most crucial choice I made to become a top achiever.

Former President Obama made a similar choice while pursuing his Master's degree at Columbia University in New York. He limited his dates and only attended a few parties, as he shares in his book Dreams From My Father. Sacrificing is a powerful tool, but everyone uses it differently. The goal is to increase our ability and willingness to sacrifice. Once I set that as my objective and worked towards it, my willingness level increased. I even started a habit of praising and rewarding myself for sacrificing so much. After a few months of sacrificing, I'd reward myself with a special 3-day trip or a visit to my country home. Constantly cheering myself on and recognizing my efforts made me proud of myself and more willing to sacrifice.

Working hard to achieve your goals may not come naturally, but it can be done! By consistently training our minds and bodies, we can reach a point where we want to work hard and miss it if we don't. Let me share two examples to illustrate this point.

Firstly, when my brother-in-law, Russell Davis, discovered that my sons weren't keen on reading, he challenged them to read some interesting literature for an hour every day for thirty days and see how they felt about it. This approach worked, and they began to enjoy reading much more.

Secondly, some of us may have heard of the term "runner's high." Runners become aware of how much they miss the pleasure of running when they skip a session. The body releases endorphins, a chemical hormone that produces a short-lasting, deeply euphoric feeling. Over time, runners become addicted to running each day, which can be healthy and fulfilling.

Using these two examples, we can train ourselves to become moderately addicted to studying and hard work. We can mold our minds to wake up each day with the goal of achieving Black Excellence. Even at my age, I wake up each day at 5:30 A.M. excited to pursue my dreams, visions, and goals. I developed this habit during my college years, and it has stayed with me ever since. I grab my coffee, nutria-bar, and banana, and head to my computer to work towards my perceived destiny of success.

In keeping with our consistent theme of always looking for the wisdom of others on our important objectives, I came across some wise words from a renowned Black author, Malcolm Gladwell, in his bestselling book "Outliers." Gladwell suggests that deliberate or intentional practice is more effective than just going through the motions. To illustrate his point, he uses golf training as an example. Instead of simply hitting two buckets of balls each day, he advises picking a specific spot on the course and tracking how many balls land in that circle. By measuring your progress each day and keeping a record, you can document your improvement over time. This advice aligns with the philosophy of Jack Welch, a famous modern-day businessman who once said, "If it's not worth measuring, then it's not worth doing!" I have personally applied Gladwell's principle to my academic learning drills in SAT tests, vocabulary, and other areas, and have found that it works wonders.

Perform Your Hard Work With Determination and Tenacity!

When two equally skilled individuals compete for a position or an outcome, the one with the most determination and tenacity tends to come out on top. This has been my experience not just in academics and the military, but also in sports like soccer and basketball. While talent and skill are important, it is often the tenacity and determination to succeed that make the difference between winning and losing.

But how does one develop this tenacity and determination to be a winner more often than not? While some people may naturally possess these qualities, I believe that determination and tenacity can also be taught and molded into a person's character. By setting a strong vision, belief, or goal, individuals can cultivate a tenacious spirit that helps them overcome obstacles and achieve their objectives.

I have seen examples of this in many contexts, from the Women's King movie to the Civil Rights Movement led by Dr. Martin Luther King and the Black Panther Party. These groups of people were remade and molded into determined and tenacious individuals, driven by a shared vision and sense of purpose. While not everyone may be able to muster this level of determination, I believe that it is possible to cultivate it within ourselves through practice and perseverance. By setting our sights on a clear goal and developing the discipline to pursue it relentlessly, we too can become tenacious and determined individuals who achieve great things.

Roosevelt Grier was a formidable football player for the Los Angeles Rams and Baltimore Colts in the 1960s. On the field, he was feared for his tenacity, but off the field, he had a completely different personality. He was known for his kindness and softness and enjoyed doing needlepoint knitting as a hobby, even authoring a book called "Rosey Grier's Needlepoint for Men." We can learn from Grier's example and create a double personality. We can have our authentic self when we're with friends and family, but develop a character of determination for situations such as in the military, in a competitive business, on the basketball court, or in movie scenes.

When Denzel Washington portrayed Malcolm X in the movie of the same name, he became Malcolm, taking on his persona for the role. As a young man, I quickly learned how to role-play and appear confident in situations like in the classroom, military cadet position, and track and basketball, even though I was very nervous. I became so good at role-playing that I excelled in my various activities. Allen Iverson, one of the greatest basketball players ever and a member of the Basketball Hall of Fame, revealed in a recent interview that he too was always nervous before every game, but he found a way to play through it and achieve high performance. We can also learn to play through our nervousness and develop a determined spirit to achieve our goals.

CHAPTER 4
ENEMIES AND VARIOUS POWERS ARE WORKING TO BLOCK US FROM ACCESSING AND USING OUR SUPERPOWERS

> *Some organizations and people are working to control you, make you fail, and become dependent on them so that they can become more powerful and wealthy or claim that your race is inferior to theirs. So don't let your guard down!*

Let's make something clear: not everyone wants you to succeed. Some individuals and organizations are driven by greed and do not want to share the benefits of society equally. They aim to become more prosperous and powerful and view you as a threat to their goals. Others hold a bias against you due to your Black heritage. Your adversaries believe they can best achieve their objectives by exploiting your time, money, and labor to increase their wealth and influence.

For instance, during the recent political campaign sessions, the owner of Walgreen Pharmacy encouraged people to buy their products and then donated the proceeds to radical right-wing conservative groups. These groups work against our interests, attempting to block the John Lewis voting rights bill, suppress our right to vote, deprive our needy citizens of Obamacare and other adequate health insurance, and oppose the George Floyd bill aimed at protecting us from police brutality.

Moreover, White supremacist groups hold the belief that their race is superior to all others, especially the Black race. They are unwilling to see Black individuals become top achievers or successful in any way. As a result, they work tirelessly to control our minds and actions, distract us from productive endeavors, and restrict us from accessing the superpowers available to us.

Distractions

The most significant challenge to achieving our goals and becoming Top Achievers is distractions. Distractions are anything that takes our attention away from our objectives, making it difficult to start or complete a task or goal. For instance, spending excessive amounts of time watching TV, playing video games, or engaging too much on social media platforms like Facebook, Instagram, and TikTok can be harmful distractions. In some cases, these distractions can become an addiction, preventing you from focusing on your goals. Harvard University had a situation years ago where male students became addicted to playing video games well into the night. The university had to shut down the Internet after midnight to help the students overcome their addiction.

I consider these distractions as enemies to success and limit the time I spend on them. However, I do not believe that one should give them up entirely, but instead, use them in moderation. Unfortunately, excessive use of some social media platforms has led to more severe problems than just negatively impacting success achievement. Several parents and government organizations have blamed these platforms for causing anxiety, depression, and other dangerous mental health issues, even leading to suicide. There are currently multiple lawsuits pending against TikTok and Instagram involving these charges. According to Insider News (www.insider.com), a parent of a 13-year-old girl filed a lawsuit in the U.S. District Court in Denver, Colorado, claiming that their daughter began using Facebook at age 7, leading to issues such as an eating disorder, self-harm, severe anxiety, depression, and a decrease in academic motivation. Additionally, earlier in the year, a Pennsylvania mother sued TikTok for recommending a video dare that her 10-year-old daughter tried, resulting in her death.

TikTok has also faced accusations that several children lost their lives while attempting the "Blackout Challenge."

While medical issues affecting youth are serious, there's another issue that is equally concerning - the negative impact of distractions on our youth's pursuit of their careers and life goals. According to a study from October 2021, Instagram has 1.3 billion users and TikTok has 1 billion users. The same report found that 63% of young people aged 12 to 17 use TikTok on a weekly basis. In a New York Times article published on February 27, 2023, it was reported that American teenagers typically spend about half of their waking hours on their smartphones. They use their phones when they're alone at home and when they're hanging out with friends. This is alarming news! When do they find time to read, learn about world events, become social activists, and pursue their life goals? Distractions can easily derail our lives, so let's work together - youth and adults - to manage and control these distractions.

Avoid Becoming a Modern-Day Slave, A Psychological Slave: There's A Marketing War by Your Enemies to take Control of Your Mind

I am sure you get tired of constantly trying to sort through the non-stop stream of words of advice you receive. I am equally sure it is difficult for you to decide which advice is important enough to put into practice. Be aware that hundreds of companies, groups, and people in your world want to capture and control your mind. For example, some want to train and convince you that the most important things in your life should be how you dress, to own a flashy car, to be the life of the parties and social scenes, to smoke and share your cigarettes with your buddies, to demonstrate how you can hold your booze, to show people that you can try drugs and not get hooked, and so forth. They work hard to get you hooked on the above to milk you for every penny you ever get. In short, you become their slave, not physically, but rather a "psychological slave." Becoming a psychological slave is much worse than being in physical bondage. Part of their strategy is to reduce your enthusiasm and drive. So, stay alert to all of their tactics to control your thinking. The best defense I know of is to work hard to become a knowledgeable, independent thinker with a powerful mind and competitive skills. If you study continuously, get mentors to help you, and get skills training in things like computers, the Internet, and business, you can avoid becoming someone else's psychological slave for life. Moreover, by developing valuable skills and making good academic and career choices, you will avoid becoming a pawn to be used by those hundreds of companies, groups, and people who want to make money off your weaknesses.

Procrastination

One of the most significant obstacles to success is procrastination, putting off things for later when they could easily be done right away. More formally, procrastination is unnecessarily postponing getting something accomplished, despite being aware that waiting may have some negative consequences. Let's make it our practice to do important things as soon as feasible, regardless of the anxiety and stress that we might feel. Then, when we get it completed, our joy of completing the task far outweighs the stress and anxiety we incurred getting it done.

Two classic adages capture the sense of negative outcomes of delaying actions in getting tasks completed:

1) **"A stitch in time saves nine."** This adage means that if a thread in your pants or skirt starts to unravel, it is crucial to have it re-sewn or stitched right away. If you delay, it will unravel more, eventually needing as many as nine stitches to repair it.

2) **"For want of a nail, the shoe was lost;** for want of a shoe, the horse was lost; for want of a horse the soldier was lost; for want of a soldier the war was lost!" So, the wise advice was to immediately replace the missing nail in a horse's shoe. For us, that means that we should not procrastinate.

A helpful practice to avoid procrastination is using 3 x 5 note cards. Throughout the day and night, I make a mental note of tasks I need to complete. If I don't write them down immediately, I often forget them within an hour. While my sons keep their reminders on their iPhones and computers, I prefer to keep mine on a folded 3 x 5 note card that I always have with me, either in my pocket with a pen or by my bedside. I check my note cards 10 to 15 times a day as I complete tasks, crossing them out and adding new ones as needed. This keeps me from forgetting things I want to accomplish, and I feel a sense of accomplishment several times throughout the day. Even executives at General Electric who earned over $300K a year used note cards religiously. So, why not try it for a couple of weeks? It could become a success habit for you too!

Fear of Failure: "Freedom to Fail!" Overcoming the "Fear of Failure!"

People worldwide know the famous movie actor Denzel Washington, who has won nearly every possible acting award, including the Academy Award for Best Actor. He has two sons, and one of them, John David Washington, is also an actor. From his early youth, John liked acting and was very good at it. However, John decided not to pursue it as a career because he was afraid he might not be able to live up to the high expectations that everyone had for him since he was Denzel Washington's son (fear of failure). Instead, as he attended Morehouse College, he decided to pursue a career in football. He continued enjoying acting on and off but excelled in football at Morehouse and was drafted into the National Football League (NFL). After one year, he was cut from football and decided to discuss his love of acting with his dad and his fears about taking acting as a career and trying to live up to the high expectations set by him and his fans because of his performance and achievement.

Denzel told John that people must not go through life trying to live up to other people's expectations of them. He said to do your best each time, enjoy it, have fun, and feel free to fail. Failing at a time when you did your very best is nothing to be ashamed of. Go practice more and come back stronger! Following is the quote of the statements by John and Denzel: "When asked about some of the lessons he's learned from his dad, Denzel, John, the 'Malcolm and Marie' star replied: 'The freedom to fail, to find out, flourish in that failure. In that being uncomfortable, you'll find the greatest parts of yourself as an artist.'"

Denzel Washington spoke about watching his son on film last January, admitting that it was "too weird" for him. "You know, it was too weird," the 67-year-old said about watching the sci-fi action thriller "Tenet." First, we went to Chris' house and screened it in his theater. So, I'm sitting here now and watching my son starring in a Christopher Nolan movie in Christopher Nolan's house. So, there was a lot going on, you know?" He added, "I'm looking at my son, and I'm like, 'He sounds like me.' Like, 'Of course, he sounds like you, stupid, he is…' You know, there were so many things that I was experiencing, you know, as a father."

"Fear of failure" is one of the most crippling psychological feelings when trying to perform any personal activity. Many of us have heard of outstanding academic performing students who "freeze up" when taking critical exams. I have observed that with several members of my family and friends. They become mentally frozen by the fear that they may perform poorly or not at all. Likewise, I watched a professional NBA basketball game in which the underdog team was leading by about 20 points with just a few minutes left in the game. Then they began thinking about the possibility that they might lose after all. At that point, their fear of failure caused their muscles to tighten up, and they couldn't make any more shots, even the very easy ones that they had successfully taken many times before. In the end, the other team won!

Protect Yourself from Evil People

Many good people and many evil people of all races, colors, religions, and creeds make up our world. Evil people are bad people who do not want to obey the fair laws of mankind and God relative to respecting and loving everyone, treating everyone equally, and giving everyone the freedom to decide who and what they want to be. Evil people want to take advantage of us, to use us to gain something for themselves. They want to trick us into believing that we are inferior to them, that we are not equal to them, and that they deserve to be rich while limiting our richness and freedom. Learn to discern who is evil, and avoid them as best as possible.

Being Convinced that You Don't Need to Sacrifice

Learning how to sacrifice and endure the pain that comes with it can be crucial to achieving great success. Society has powerful marketing strategies that make us addicted to things like expensive clothing, fancy cars, and luxurious living. To obtain them, we take on low-paying jobs, engage in illegal drug sales, or even drop out of school. In some cases, we become our own worst enemies by refusing to make sacrifices. However, we can take action to avoid this by learning to sacrifice or delay our gratification. Two famous Black individuals who made tremendous sacrifices, even to the point of becoming homeless for a time, are Sidney Poitier and Tyler Perry. Sidney drew upon a superpower to become an Academy Award-winning actor, one of the best of all time. Tyler Perry became a billionaire in the movie production industry, purchasing an entire military base that used to be a slave plantation. Furthermore, "Learning how to sacrifice and endure the pain that comes with it can be crucial to achieving great success!"

CHAPTER 5
"WISDOM BLOCKS" FROM AROUND THE WORLD TO HELP YOU ACHIEVE YOUR POTENTIAL GREATNESS

As stated in previous chapters of this book, my significant successes in life are a result of seeking, accepting, and implementing the wisdom gained from elders, teachers, business leaders, religious figures, and more. The knowledge I gained was not always complete, but rather came in small pieces, which I refer to as "wisdom blocks." In this book, I am passing on some of those blocks, including ones I formulated and successfully used during my journey towards success. I strongly recommend that you formally incorporate the process of collecting, evaluating, and utilizing selected "wisdom blocks" in your development towards success. Here are some of the most important ones:

Return the Favors

When someone invests their time and effort in your success, commit to finding a way to reciprocate by helping them as much or more in achieving their goals. I turned this step into a creative and challenging game for myself, always searching for articles, information, and advice that I could share with one or more of my supporters.

Visit the Elderly and Ask Them to Tell You About Their Life Struggles and Successes

When you invest your time and effort in supporting others, it can make them feel happy and appreciated. This can help build a strong relationship, where they are more likely to reciprocate and support you in achieving your goals. By taking the time to understand their needs and challenges, you can gain valuable insights and advice that can contribute to your success. In turn, they may also consider you as part of their legacy and continue to offer valuable guidance and support. So, make it a habit to go out of your way to help others, and you may find that it comes back to you in unexpected and rewarding ways.

Look at Career and Business Opportunities in Both a Visionary/ Strategic and Tactical Manner

AI (Artificial Intelligence) is currently a prominent and widely used scientific technology by companies like Amazon, Google, and others. It may surprise many business leaders to learn that I founded and operated an AI company in the 1970s with several global clients. Back then, I researched the topic thoroughly and found it very promising for the future. I aimed to develop a smaller, practical application for immediate use and formed an LLC corporation named AI Services Company. In addition to serving major software application-oriented clients, I held AI training seminars across Connecticut, California, and Canada. The point I want to make is that I investigated every opportunity from a futuristic perspective and sought to implement an aspect of it in a limited, practical way to generate income.

Consciously Manage Your Career Dreams

Having or formulating career dreams is critically important. For instance, if you work at McDonald's or any other entry-level job and base all your hopes and plans on performing more efficiently, earning small pay increases faster, and working longer hours, you're selling yourself short. Of course, it's crucial to execute your current duties to the best of your abilities every day. Nevertheless, overly focusing on your current role can lead to stagnation and hinder your progress towards potential future successes. It's essential to dream and imagine what your future might hold. Nonetheless, as the renowned black movie mogul, Denzel Washington once said,

"Remember, a dream is just a dream." To achieve your aspirations, setting goals and devising plans is vital.

Always Look to Turn Your Setbacks into Comebacks or Opportunities!

In recent years, I have grown more and more confident in my abilities, to the point where I began to think that I could do anything. So, about a month ago, I decided to trim a tall tree in front of my house and climbed a 15-foot ladder to do so, despite warnings from my wife and children not to do so at the age of 79. I sneaked up the ladder and did a great job trimming the tree. But as I started to climb down, the ladder began to fall to one side. Being overly optimistic, I jumped off the ladder, thinking I could fly, and ended up landing on my right foot, breaking it and losing my driving privileges for six weeks. What a terrible setback! Now I'm confined to my home. But how can I turn this into an opportunity? The result is this book. It's such a great result that I'm considering buying another 15-foot ladder (smiles). Have you experienced any setbacks in your life? There's an adage that goes, "When life gives you lemons, don't complain; start a lemonade business." (I'm paraphrasing.) Michael Jordan, for example, was cut from his high school basketball team in 10th grade. Rather than quitting, he used his disappointment and anger to become a significantly better player, ultimately becoming one of the greatest basketball players in history.

Discover a Way to Make Yourself Constantly Positive, Cheerful, and Confident

We have all seen cheerleaders at football and basketball games. Even when their teams are losing badly, the cheerleaders jump and yell, telling the players that they can still win the game! That often motivates the team to go all out and return to win. We all need cheerleaders in our personal lives. However, most of us cannot afford to hire one to encourage us, and even if we did, they would not be with us every day and night when we might have to go through tough times. I discovered a bible verse and a song that gave me some good advice: "encourage yourself;" that is, become your own cheerleader. The following are lyrics from that song: "Sometimes you have to encourage yourself. Sometimes you have to speak victory during the test!" (Donald Lawrence, The Tri-City Singers)

Based on that advice, I learned and practiced becoming my own best cheerleader. The good news is that I am always with myself to cheer myself on and with no significant expenses. I encourage you to do the same. Two superhuman NFL Super Bowl quarterbacks, Jalen Hurts and Patrick Mahomes, are currently using an alternative approach. Following are quotes from each:

Hurts said his faith had carried him through some tough seasons, including being benched after his freshman year at the University of Alabama. "I understand that God put those obstacles and challenges in my life for a reason. He wanted me to feel the pain I felt for a reason. He wanted me to understand the importance of never losing faith and always staying true to myself. He had not brought me this far to leave me there."

On a similar note, Mahomes told KMBC-TV, "My Christian faith plays a role in everything I do. I ask God to lead me in the right direction and let me be who I am in His name." It has a role in everything I do, and obviously, He'll be on the big stage in the Super Bowl that He's given me, and I want to make sure I'm glorifying Him while I do it." If you are not a "person of faith," you can still become your own cheerleader and get great results in motivating yourself.

> *"If you are not a "person of faith," you indeed can become your own cheerleader and get great results in motivating yourself."*

Emphasize Family Legacy Accomplishments:

One of the greatest gifts from my mother to my eleven siblings and I was the gift of confidence and pride-building. She said that we were exceptional and very talented people. She spoke with pride about the accomplishments of our relatives, pointing out that one of our cousins was the President of the local Black bank, and another cousin worked under Supreme Court Justice Thurgood Marshall on the Brown versus Board of Education case. In contrast, two Virginia and North Carolina cousins were famous Pastors, and several others were highly successful. Yes, we were taught that success was in our genes, our DNA. As a result, we twelve children grew up believing in the great opportunities possible in our future lives. It is so crucial that our Black youth are taught self-pride, believing that each can have access to unique gifts from God, irrespective of their past or current conditions or situations. Let us Black adults give them the gift of self-confidence and pride. Hopefully, this book will assist in achieving that objective.

Avoid Becoming a Modern-Day Slave, A Psychological Slave Because There's A Marketing War to take Control of Your Mind!

I am sure you are tired of constantly trying to sort through the non-stop stream of advice you receive. It can be difficult to decide which advice is important enough to put into practice. Be aware that there are many groups of people in your world who want to control your mind. Some want to convince you that the most important things in life are how you dress, owning a flashy car, being the life of the party, demonstrating how well you can hold your booze or try drugs without getting hooked, and so forth. They work hard to get you hooked on these things to milk you for every penny you ever get. In short, you become their slave, not physically, but rather a "psychological slave," which can be much worse than physical bondage. So, make sure that you stay alert to what is happening to your mind! The best defense is to work hard to become a knowledgeable, independent thinker with a powerful mind and a set of competitive skills. By developing valuable skills and making good academic and career choices, you can avoid becoming a pawn to be used by hundreds of companies, groups, and people who want to make money off your weaknesses.

Strive to Become Content in Life

During my youth and early adulthood, I viewed the word "contentment" in a negative light. I believed that it meant being satisfied with one's accomplishments and simply resigning oneself to a state of relaxation. To me, it seemed like a term that described laziness. However, about a decade ago, our Associate Pastor, Rev. Dr. Hargrove, in Rockville, MD, discussed this term with us during a Bible study class. She pointed out that the Apostle Paul stated in the biblical Book of Philippians 4:11-12 that "In every circumstance, I have learned to be content." What he meant was that he had learned to maintain a positive, thankful, and appreciative attitude under all circumstances, whether good or bad. Since then, I have made a conscious effort to do the same and encourage you to do so as well.

Read! Read! Read!

You can buy the most powerful computer in the world, but if you don't put any data into it, nothing will come out. As the old saying goes, "garbage in, garbage out!" That's why it's crucial to read a lot of high-quality material on various topics as often as possible. Listening, watching, and thinking are also closely related to reading. Recently, I came across a relevant quote from an unknown source: "You become what you read. You become what you listen to. You become what you watch. You become what you think. Choose wisely." It's a powerful reminder to be selective and mindful of the content we consume.

"No Pain, No Gain!"

Many people wake up each day with their dreams and goals, and give 90 to 100 percent effort. But given the obstacles, oppression, and barriers I faced daily, I resolved to outdo them and give 125 percent! I would work half of each Saturday, go to church on Sunday, and devote the remaining time to achieving my goals. Yes, it was a sacrifice and painful, but it brought me a tremendous sense of accomplishment and joy. And, more often than not, I achieved remarkable success while remaining at peace and happy. As the saying goes, "Lots of pain, lots of gain!"

Good and Evil People Come in All Colors. Race is Not the Determining Factor

Currently, there's a lot of discussion about Critical Race Theory (CRT). Governors of Florida, Virginia, and other states are arguing, seemingly for political reasons, that teaching about race in schools is detrimental. They claim that topics like Black Lives

Matter, reparations, or sexual identity will promote hatred among Black and White students. However, teaching facts and the truth is always healthy for everyone. If factual and truthful education about CRT is not taught in schools, Black parents should take the initiative to teach their children and grandchildren about it. My parents taught me to be wary of White people, but that there are also wonderful White people, like the Esters family, who supported our family's success. They rented us a home and leased farmland to grow crops on in a sharecropper arrangement, and were very understanding and lenient on payment terms. My dad also taught me to be aware of bad people in general, regardless of race.

Nevertheless, my distrust of all White people persisted until I joined the United States Air Force in Omaha, Nebraska in 1967. As a young Second Lieutenant arriving on the Air Force Base, I was greeted by my assigned mentor, First Lieutenant Donald Kingsley, a White man from Alexandria, Virginia. Don welcomed me warmly, briefed me on my upcoming military life, and treated me like a brother. He introduced me to his loving wife Tammy and later to his parents, Mom and Dad Kingsley. They even chose me to be the godfather of their first child, Donald Jr., and I essentially became a true member of their family in Alexandria.

I became friends with Don's siblings, Michael and Karen, and I still maintain those friendships today. Mom and Dad Kingsley became marriage and family mentors to my wife and me, and they cherished our three children. Our relationship transcended race, and I am forever grateful to Don and his family for changing my view of White people. Two of my in-laws are White, and one is Mexican, and there is no one in the world better than they are. I love them dearly. Race is not the basis for evil.

Build and Constantly Enhance Your Support Network Team: To Strive for High Achievement

No one person can build an automobile or win a war. Success depends on assembling a great team and getting them committed to the accomplishment of a great goal. When I was young, I realized that I had no money or resources to achieve anything significant on my own. To accomplish my dreams, I needed to convince others to support and work with me. I recognized that the Elders in my village had a wealth of knowledge and wisdom, so I spent time talking and listening to them. They appreciated my time and grew to like me, becoming fully committed to helping me reach my goals. Looking back, I can see how our chats made them feel valued and appreciated. When someone invests their time and resources in your success, you should commit to helping them achieve their goals. I challenged myself to provide articles, advice, and examples to everyone in my support network, making it a creative and rewarding game for me.

Develop a Mantra or Victory Chant for Yourself

Some people find it beneficial to create a personal rally-cry, a call to arms, a chant, or a mantra to motivate themselves to strive for high achievement. When used often, it can become emotional and make one excited. Positive self-talk, such as "You can do it!" or well-known mantras like Nike's "Just Do It!" or Kobe Bryant's "Black Mamba Mentality" can help build a mentality of determination. In my conversations with my sister Anne Hairston France, we discussed ways to motivate ourselves through difficult times and obstacles to achieve significant accomplishments. Our common mantra became "In Spite Of!" Anne faced numerous obstacles, but she was determined to overcome them and be successful "In Spite Of" them. I adopted that mantra and continue to use it to motivate myself to achieve.

Develop Yourself into a Leader. Leaders are Not All "Natural Born-Leaders."

Leaders in all areas of our society are highly valued and paid for, whether in business, education, military, politics, sports, or otherwise. Certain people appear to have leadership traits from early childhood, lasting throughout adulthood. As a consequence, some people assume that those who don't have natural leadership traits cannot become great leaders. That is not true! If it were true, you would not have the great work and results of leadership building of thousands of military leaders at the West Point Academy, the Naval Academy, and other military academies. Together, they enroll over 13,000 young military students each year to develop them into leaders. So, most of us can become leaders if we want to and strive to do so.

Live Each Day with Intentionality and Tenacity

My son Charles recently shared a "Wisdom Block" he found, and I will keep the source anonymous. The message goes like this: "Having intentions (goals) in everything you do is crucial. It doesn't have to be grand. Just having intent. Intent to gain knowledge. Intent to finish a project. Intent to elevate your jump. Intent to enhance your writing or speaking skills. Intent! Intent! Intent! It's the destination at the intersection of Will and Want Avenue!"

CHAPTER 6
URGENT CALL TO ACTION: WE MUST CONTINUE THE FIGHT FOR EQUAL RIGHTS, OPPORTUNITIES AND JUSTICE FOR BLACK AMERICANS!

As Black enslavement in America began over 400 years ago, it is clear that the progress towards equal rights, opportunities, and justice for Black people has been too slow and insufficient. Despite notable landmarks like the Emancipation Proclamation in 1865 and the Civil Rights Act in 1964, each step forward has been met with a White Supremacist counter-move to slow or stop progress. For instance, the Jim Crow policies and laws implemented in Southern states after the Emancipation Proclamation were designed to take away new freedoms and deny job opportunities to Black people. The Vagrancy Law further enabled the White landowners to rent out incarcerated Blacks for pennies. Similarly, after the passing of the Civil Rights Act, White Supremacists took immediate actions to suppress and minimize Black and Brown votes, using drug violations and other reasons to imprison them and strip them of their voting rights. Over 30 pieces of state legislation under review aim to suppress the right to vote throughout the

United States. Recently, on March 5, 2023, President Joe Biden spoke at the Edmund Pettus Bridge in Selma, Alabama, where in 1965 civil rights marchers were attacked by police to keep them from protesting voter suppression and denial. Biden stressed that voting, a "fundamental right," remains under assault from conservative Supreme Court justices, state lawmakers, and election deniers. While steps have been taken to address the issue, he urged Congress to pass new voting legislation named after the late Georgia Rep. John Lewis, who suffered a skull fracture during "Bloody Sunday."

The lack of progress in achieving equal rights, opportunities, and justice for Black people in America has been disappointing and frustrating. This has led some Black individuals to take drastic steps to cope with their negative or angry feelings. For instance, some Black people with fair or White complexions have decided to "pass as White" to enjoy White privilege, while others have formed social movements such as the "Back to Africa Movement" led by Marcus Garvey. Some outstanding Black achievers have also lost hope and moved to foreign countries, such as France, known for its reputation of being hospitable to Black people.

However, as one team of warriors gets tired, another fresh set of fighters always joins the battle to keep hope alive. These new warriors include Dr. Martin Luther King Jr., Fannie Lou Hamer, Barbara Jordan, John Lewis, Medgar Evers, Rev. Al Sharpton, Stacey Abrams, James Clyburn, and Rev. Raphael Warnock, among many others. The struggle is far from over, and as President Biden said, we must remain vigilant. It is critical to elect Senate and House members who support us and can help pass the necessary new laws.

Unfortunately, some states that oppose us use voter suppression tactics to prevent us from getting the number of votes we need to pass the bills. However, it is worth noting that only 67 percent of eligible U.S. voters actually vote. Therefore, if we can convince or incentivize 90 percent of Black and Brown voters to vote, we will have enough votes to pass the Voting Rights bills and equal justice and opportunities bills that are needed.

Again, our work is far from complete! We have not been able to pass the George Floyd or John Lewis Voting Rights bills, among other areas where progress has been lacking. What can we do? The U.S. population numbers are not in our favor, with Whites comprising 76 percent and Blacks only 14 percent. However, there is hope, as many White people have joined our fight for equality. Yet, we still face a significant challenge, as too many

Blacks and Whites are too passive or afraid to join our struggle. They choose not to be activists, not even to vote in federal, state, or local elections. This makes it urgent for us to devise additional strategies to keep making progress. As I pondered this challenge, I thought of the remarkable work of red ants in the deserts of Phoenix, Arizona and Scandinavia. We can learn a lot from their actions and determination. Each tiny ant understood the benefits of having a tall ant hill, which would provide better food storage and shelter. But, individually, they were not optimistic, knowing that their little effort alone would not build a several-foot-high ant hill. Nevertheless, they were willing to contribute to building a smaller ant hill. I read a newspaper article recently that reported a Swedish man discovered a tall ant hill in 2021, with 300,000 red ants inside that had built a 9-foot-tall anthill. Amazing! Similarly, many Blacks don't believe they have any power, and that it is not worth voting. What if we could encourage them to identify with the red ants and join us in building a 9-foot-high hill of Black voting power to put more political leaders in place to promote equality for all Americans? Let's work to recruit every young voting-age Black person, every incarcerated Black person, every Black homeless person, and so on, and get them to join our red ant force for equality. We can even pay them to become recruiters and take our training classes on activism, justice, and fairness. It is essential to test them on these subjects to ensure they are well-trained to recruit all of the "ants/individuals" in their community groups. Yes, let's charge forward! Don't wait for progress to happen on its own. Let's strive for more progress. Charge forward to transform yourself into a self-made Top Achiever, a social activist, a "drum major" for equality and justice for all. Experiment with some of the ideas and suggestions in this book, but also read, research, and find other means to achieve your potential destiny of success, as well as success for all of us as Black people—God-endowed Black Excellence!

ACKNOWLEDGEMENTS

The pace of life can feel incredibly fast-moving and non-stop, especially if you're someone who is highly inquisitive and blessed with boundless energy. That's certainly true for me. Most mornings, I'm up bright and early at around 5:30 A.M., grabbing a cup of coffee before settling in at my computer for some research and study. As much as I've enjoyed the thrill of this rollercoaster life, it's also kept me from developing the discipline I needed to write the books I've always dreamed of.

Fortunately, I've been blessed with a lot of wonderful people in my life who've kept the pressure on me to slow down and make good on my promise to write one or two books. Many of my former students from both the Bachelor's and Master's degree programs at Nyack College-Washington, DC Campus have been especially insistent. During late nights of teaching, I've tried to impart wisdom about their careers and life in general. They've been receptive to my teachings, and many have urged me to compile them into a book.

Now, after much encouragement, I'm thrilled to announce that my two books on my life journey and one about the lessons I've learned will soon be available. I'm grateful to all of those who've supported and pushed me along the way. My wife Indira and children Tanya, Jason, and Charles have been incredible sources of encouragement and support. My siblings, particularly Thelma and Anne, my brother-in-law George France, and my granddaughter Kami have also been instrumental in editing and supporting my work.

I'm thankful for my many friends who have taken the time to speak with me and offer their encouragement. And, last but not least, I'd like to express my gratitude to my dear friend and former student, Dr. Bryon J. Williams, for his ongoing support, monthly calls, and willingness to write the Forward for me. I'm also incredibly grateful for my formal book editor and marketer, Ms. Tamika Woodard of TJW Enterprises, LLC, who has tirelessly assisted me with editing and book publishing.

OUR RECOMMENDED SOURCES OF FACTS, KNOWLEDGE, WISDOM AND ADVICE

Uncle Tom's Cabin

Harriet Beecher Stowe's 1851 novel, "Uncle Tom's Cabin," bravely exposed the inhumane practice of slavery of Black people in the United States. Stowe, who grew up in a devoutly Christian family in a northern, slave-free state, was ahead of her time in bringing attention to the immoralities of slavery. However, the novel was banned in the southern slave-holding states, much like the current censorship efforts of Governor DeSantis and others in 2023.

To Kill a Mockingbird

Harper Lee's 1960 novel, "To Kill a Mockingbird," is a classic piece of American literature that tackles the crisis of racial discrimination and the low status of Black people in a southern town. The story centers on a White lawyer who risks his career to defend an innocent Black man. The novel delves into the roots and consequences of racism and prejudice, exploring how good and evil can exist within a single community or individual.

Caste

Isabel Wilkerson's "Caste" is a Pulitzer Prize-winning, factual book that provides a comprehensive look into racial oppression and cruelty towards Blacks and others through the implementation of a caste system. It explores the intentional strategy of White Supremacists to separate people by race, the color of their skin, and other key criteria enforced by cruelty and even lynchings. Though it can be a difficult and emotionally painful read, "Caste" is a must-read book that sheds light on the oppressive nature of systemic racism.

The Woman King Film

Set in West Africa during the 1800s, this film is based on a true story in which an all-female group of Black warriors fought fiercely to defend their African Kingdom of Dahomey against a formidable French army. It showcases Black excellence at its finest.

True History: The Legacy of Jim Crow

This informative book delves into the creation and ongoing practice of Jim Crow in America. Written by Clarence A. Haynes, the book is easily understandable for younger readers but also offers new insights for adults. Despite my extensive reading background at the age of 80, I learned many details that were previously unknown to me.

A Raisin in the Sun by Lorraine Hansberry

The story depicts a Black family's struggle to improve their financial situation in south Chicago following the father's death. It addresses themes of housing discrimination, racism, and assimilation. A central message of the play is that even in the face of oppression and financial struggles, families can achieve their dreams if they remain united.

I Am Not Your Negro, a Documentary Film by Raoul Peck

This exceptional documentary focuses primarily on the fight for racial and economic justice during the 1950s, 60s, and 70s, providing valuable insight into the ongoing struggle against racial hatred. At the center of this explosive documentary is my favorite author, essayist, and political activist James Baldwin. In the late

1980s, just before his death, Baldwin had planned to write a book called Remember This House, which dealt with the civil rights activities and successive assassinations of Medgar Evers, Malcolm X, and Martin Luther King Jr. Unfortunately, he only managed to complete 30 or so pages of that planned book. This documentary seeks to imagine what else he would have said. It conveys the hatred, violence, and prejudice which several featured Black men faced in their various leadership roles. Additionally, it uses archival footage of the Civil Rights movement as a bridge to the current racial flare-ups and the response of the #BlackLivesMatter movement. Sadly, police in both eras have used excessive violence against unarmed Black men, women, and children. Credit: www.spirituality.com

Black Panther, a Movie Featuring Chadwick Boseman

As Black people, this movie holds significant importance to us as it showcases the beauty of the African continent and the brilliance, grace, and power of the Black race. The Black Panther movie garnered seven Academy Award nominations, including Best Picture, and won three. But what exactly made Black Panther such a groundbreaking film? A significant amount of its praise stems from its race- and gender-conscious casting and costuming. It boasts the Marvel Cinematic Universe's first Black director, Ryan Coogler; an almost entirely Black lead cast; and several Black women in powerful and engaging roles. Encyclopedia Britannica deserves credit for this insight.

Letter From the Birmingham Jail, Written by Rev. Dr. Martin Luther King, Jr.

The "Letter from Birmingham Jail," also known as the "Letter from Birmingham City Jail" and "The Negro Is Your Brother," is an open letter written by Dr. King on April 16, 1963. In it, he asserted that people have a moral responsibility to break unjust laws and to take non-violent direct action to correct them, rather than waiting potentially forever for justice to come through the courts. Responding to being referred to as an "outsider," King wrote, "Injustice anywhere is a threat to justice everywhere." He wrote the letter in response to a "Call for Unity" by the local White Clergy and White city leadership. The letter has been described as "one of the most important historical documents written by a modern political prisoner" and is considered a classic document of civil disobedience. I have read this document several times, and I plan to read it again. The information was sourced from Wikipedia.

The Willie Lynch Letter, and The Making of a Slave

The William Lynch speech, also known as the Willie Lynch letter, is a speaking presentation delivered by a White Racist, William Lynch, to an audience of White slave-owners on the banks of the James River in Virginia in 1712 regarding how to better control their slaves. The letter describes how to mold and control the minds of the slaves to get them to accept their condition of slavery. These techniques are still being tried today to control our minds. Many people say that Lynch's recipe for keeping slaves enslaved and happy are the same tactics being used today to mold the minds of Black people, and keep them psychologically enslaved and happy.

Dreams From My Father, by President Barack Obama

Dreams from My Father: A Story of Race and Inheritance (1995) is a book by President Obama that explores the events of his early childhood in Hawaii, his years in Chicago until his entry into Harvard Law School in 1988. Obama originally published his memoir in 1995, when he was starting his political campaign to become the U.S. Senator representing the state of Illinois. After Obama won the Democratic Primary race in 2004, the book was re-published that year. According to The New York Times,

Obama modeled Dreams from My Father on the Black author Ralph Ellison's novel Invisible Man. This book describes the struggles, obstacles, and success steps that President Obama had to go through to ultimately become a Black Top Achiever.

The New Jim Crow, by Michelle Alexander

The New Jim Crow is a stunning account of the rebirth of a caste-like system in the United States, resulting in millions of African Americans locked behind bars and relegated to a permanent second-class status—denied the very rights supposedly won in the Civil Rights Movement. Since its publication in 2010, the book has appeared on the New York Times bestseller list for more than a year; it has been dubbed the "secular bible of a new social movement" by numerous commentators. The New Jim Crow tells a truth our nation has been reluctant to face.

The New Jim Crow is an eye-opening book that exposes the harsh reality of racial discrimination in the United States. Michelle Alexander does an excellent job of detailing how the criminal justice system targets black men and how this system of racial control perpetuates the notion of white supremacy in America. The book is a must-read for anyone who wants to understand the history of systemic racism in the United States and its lasting impact on communities of color.

Overall, these four works - Black Panther, Letter From the Birmingham Jail, Dreams From My Father, and The New Jim Crow - are all significant pieces of literature that shed light on different aspects of the Black experience. Whether it's celebrating Black culture and excellence, speaking truth to power, sharing personal stories of struggle and triumph, or exposing systemic injustice, these works have all made an impact in their own way.

2 Important Videos

Funeral Services of a Church in South Carolina Where Seven Church Members Were Killed by a White Supremacist.

This video documents the funeral services of the seven church members who were killed in a church in South Carolina by a white supremacist. It's a solemn reminder of the ongoing struggle against racial hatred and violence in our society.

I've Been to the Mountaintop, by Dr. Martin Luther King

Dr. Martin Luther King's iconic speech, "I've Been to the Mountaintop," is a powerful and inspiring message that still resonates today. It reminds us of the importance of standing up for justice and equality, even in the face of adversity.

Video Service of Funeral Service of Tyree Nichols (Rev Al Sharpton)

In this video, Rev. Al Sharpton delivers a sermon at the funeral service of Tyree Nichols. He emphasizes the point that Black people can suffer from evil and cruelty even at the hands of Black policemen. This reinforces the message from the above Caste book that a caste system often perpetuates such evils, where one group believes it can take advantage of a lower caste. In this case, the "police caste" believes it is superior to poor Black people and can be cruel to Black people without facing serious punishment. It's a poignant reminder that systemic racism still exists in our society.

Video of a Sunday Sermon at Howard University Rankin Chapel by Rev. Dr. Dante Quick

Rev. Dr. Dante Quick is an accomplished scholar and social justice advocate. In this video, his sermon titled "Bustin Loose" features the musical group Chuck Brown and the Soul Searchers. The sermon takes us through the history of Black top achiever activism and calls on each of us to engage in activism as well. The video is available on www.YouTube.com.

The Fire Next Time, by James Baldwin

"The Fire Next Time" is a masterpiece by James Baldwin, one of my favorite authors. Published in 1963, it became a national bestseller that year. It came at a time when the civil rights movement was just beginning to take root in America and gave a passionate voice to that emerging movement. Today, it still provides insight into race relations in America and is recognized as a classic work on the Black racial struggle.

When God Winks, by Best-selling Author Squire Rushnell

For those who believe in God's existence and continuous presence in their lives, "When God Winks" provides guidance on how to build intuition, discernment, meditation, introspection, and an ability to seek and accept extrasensory guidance from God or the Universe. In some sense, it seems like this book will help us learn how to access the God-offered Superpowers widely discussed in this book. The author's central message is that no matter what is happening in our lives or how uncertain things may seem at the moment, God is with us and will help us move toward success. The book's theme is that God often sends us signs to let us know that we are on the right track and that things will be okay.

ABOUT THE AUTHOR

Professor George C. Hairston was born in 1943 in Cascade, Virginia, a small town known for tobacco and vegetable farming. He grew up as the eleventh child in a family of twelve in a tobacco sharecropping and segregated economic structure. Despite attending a two-room elementary school and having no thoughts of attending college, Professor Hairston's outstanding support team of family, friends, and elders encouraged him to attend Howard University in Washington, DC. He graduated with a Bachelor of Arts in Mathematics and Philosophy and a Commission of Second

Lieutenant in the U.S. Air Force. Professor Hairston continued his education while serving in the Air Force and earned a Master's Degree in Mathematics from Creighton University. After leaving the Air Force as a Captain with an Honorable Discharge, he completed Doctoral studies at the University of Maryland and George Washington University with an A.B.D. Doctoral Degree.

Professor Hairston held Executive Leadership positions at General Electric, Honeywell, and other large companies. He was a Teaching Professor and Director of Student Recruitment at Nyack College-DC Campus, as well as the Founder and President of several corporations. In addition to his professional work, Professor Hairston is the Founder and Executive Director of Success Warriors, Inc., a Charitable Youth- and Education-focused Non-profit organization, and Hairston Enterprises, LLC, whose principal business is Education Consulting and Meeting Facilitation. He is also the Executive Director of Vision2Excel, a Career Coaching Service for both Youth and Adults.

As a former staff member of Nyack College-DC Campus, Professor Hairston served as the Student Career Development and Recruitment Leader and Lead Adjunct Professor, teaching Master's Degree Organizational Leadership, Strategic Management, Statistics, Math, Thesis Writing, and other Management courses.

He was awarded the Nyack College DC Campus 2005 Outstanding Professor of the Year and was voted "Most Creative" and "Most Caring" Professor for 2005.

Currently, Professor Hairston is the Co-Founder and Chief Operating Officer of AI Optimize, LLC, a Technology Consulting company, and Sports & Image, LLC, a NIL Agency. Professor Hairston's life is a testament to his belief in identifying one's God-given superpower and striving for excellence.

REFERENCES

Wikipedia contributors. (2023, April 13). Johari window. In Wikipedia, The Free Encyclopedia. Retrieved 14:30, April 13, 2023, from https://en.wikipedia.org/wiki/Johari_window

Hubspot. (2021). SWOT Analysis [Digital image]. Retrieved from https://blog.hubspot.com/marketing/swot-analysis-examples.